**WORKBOOKS FOR DYSLEXICS**

# Reversals

## Circle Letters in the Box

# 20 Activities

## Improve Letter Naming and Letter Writing in Children with Dyslexia

Name: _____    Date:_____

Circle all the D letters you can find in the box below.

```
        C       D    V
                              D
   W    H    D
            R
 F
      D  X   G    D      L
              O
      S L D A  D  Q   S
          D                I
      D C  M  Z  B
           P
```

Name: _____  Date: _____

Circle all the B letters you can find in the box below.

```
    B      F    V
  Y    H       D    L
          O
R    A       M    R   B
  G  B
         B    S    E
       D
  S  T    V  B   I  H   S
    B
    A  C  M    B   I
           P   Z      B
```

3

Name: _____    Date:_____

Circle all the P letters you can find in the box below.

L  E  P  V
  W  O  U  P
R  P  M  R  B
G  K  S  C
    P
S  X  G  B  I  H  S
  B  D
E  C  P  B  I
    P  G  P

4

Name: _____   Date: _____

Circle all the R letters you can find in the box below.

E I P L M
R U V
R P S V C
P
G V D
K R I R
R G B
B T S
D
N C P S G R R
G P

Name: _____  Date:_____

Circle all the M letters you can find in the box below.

E M N L M
I M U V
P S M P
Q K M
G R D
G S R I
B S G T S
N C D M S G R
M A P

Name: _____  Date: _____

Circle all the t letters you can find in the box below.

Name: _____  Date:_____

Circle all the m letters you can find in the box below.

d s m l S
e s t n V t
m t p r o c
r h P r d
s w l
g d t S
b g e m
c t h l
n m g a o P

Name: _____  Date:_____

Circle all the s letters you can find in the box below.

u m l j s t
  x     v
e s n r   c
  t   s
r   p o r s
s q   s
  w t s
g         
p e y h l
  c t   m a
n s     o p

Name: _____   Date:_____

Circle all the a letters you can find in the box below.

r t a j s t
x g a
e l r c
r a p
s t v
p r s
s a a o
b t j
w
p t y
a h l
c e a
n s m o p

Name: _____  Date: _____

Circle all the q letters you can find in the box below.

Name: _____  Date: _____

Circle all the J letters you can find in the box below.

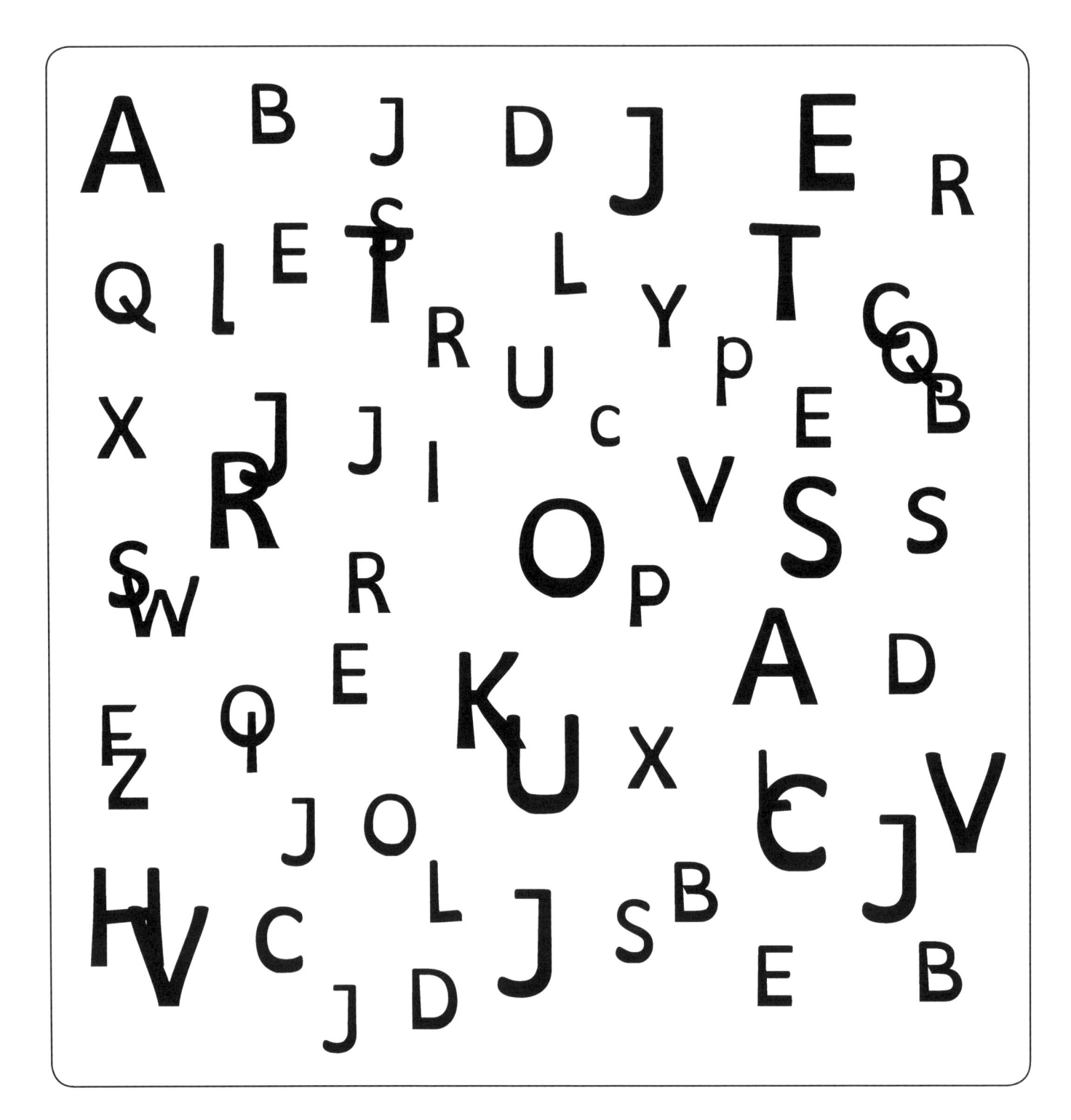

A B J D J E R
Q I E T L Y T C
R U P E B
X J J I C E
R V S S
S W R O P
E K A D
E Q U X V
Z J O E J
H V C L J S B
J D E B

12

Name: _____  Date: _____

Circle all the R letters you can find in the box below.

A B J R J E R
Q T S L T C
R T L X O B
X R U P E
J J I C V R S
R O P A D
S W R
E Q E K U X E J V
R J O L A
H V C L J S B
J R E B

Name: _____  Date:_____

Circle all the p letters you can find in the box below.

14

Name: _____  Date:_____

Circle all the q letters you can find in the box below.

Name: _____  Date:_____

Circle all the b letters you can find in the box below.

16

Name: _____  Date:_____

Circle all the d letters you can find in the box below.

17

Name: _____   Date:_____

Circle all the ƒ letters you can find in the box below.

Name: _____  Date:_____

Circle all the t letters you can find in the box below.

Name: _____  Date:_____

Circle all the m letters you can find in the box below.

20

Name: _____  Date:_____

Circle all the w letters you can find in the box below.

21

# Downhill Publishing LLC
# SINGLE USER LICENSE

Congratulations! You have purchased a great educational software one easy-to-use package!

Our Software is sold under FIVE different license agreements:
- Single User
- Unlimited School and District License
- Small Publisher (TPT)
- Large Publisher
- Digital

**By purchasing the Single User** license you may install the enclosed software ON A SINGLE computer at school and/or on a computer at home. You may NOT network the SOFTWARE or otherwise use it on more than one computer at the same time.

A SINGLE computer at school and/or on a computer at home.

If you are enthusiastic about our software, share the excitement but don't just pass it on to a friend. If your school considers to be a benefit, an Unlimited School Site License will enable all school staff to use this program (at school and at home- see information attached).

Again thanks for honoring your legal commitment by installing this software on one computer at school and one computer at home only.

Downhill Publishing LLC
80 Eighth Avenue, Suite Mezz-2
New York, NY 10011
Phone: (800) 203 0612 • FAX: (212) 661-5757

Keep this legal license for your records:
**SINGLE USER LICENSE No. F4TSUL-NY410588**
(Unlimited School and Wide District Licenses are available for ALL schools on your district. Please contact us.)

# 100% Rebate- Rebate form

Dear Teacher,

Thank you for buying this software, which provides critical tools for more effective instruction. If you are licensed as a Single User, please honor your software legal commitment by using the software on one (1) computer at school and one (1) computer at home only.

If you like the program/s, please share your enthusiasm and excitement with your supervisors and colleagues.

**If your school decides to PURCHASE* the UNLIMITED LICENSE of our software, YOU WILL BE reimbursed 100% of your purchase.***

All you have to do is:
1. Fill out this Rebate Form
2. Make a copy of your invoice
3. Email, mail, or fax it to us

REBATE ARE BASED UPON SINGLE-USER LICENSE ONLY.
*In order to get your 100% REBATE, YOUR SCHOOL MUST PURCHASE THE UNLIMITED SCHOOL LICENSE.
We accept PURCHASE ORDERS.

Your Name: _____

Your Address: _____ City: _____ State: _____ ZIP: _____

Your School Name: _____

Your School Address: _____ City: _____ State: _____ ZIP: _____

Your School P.O. Number: _____

Your invoice number: _____ Your reimbursement: $ _____

*Allow 4 weeks for reimbursement. Limit one reimbursement per school. Rebate is for the cost of the software (shipping cost is not reimbursed).

Downhill Publishing LLC • 80 Eighth Avenue, Suite Mezz 2 • New York, NY 10011
Phone: (800) 203 0612 • FAX: (212) 661-5757
www.downhillpublishing.com • info@downhillpublishing.com

A friendly message from **Downhill Publishing.**

As seen on commercial publications, this is a polite message from the company who invested a huge amount of time in making this content. Please do no make illegal copies of our copyrighted software.

Duplication, replication or file-sharing of all or any part is prohibited. This software is intended for personal use, as a **single license user**.

If you are enthusiastic about our software, share the excitement, but we ask that you don't pass it on to a friend or colleague. If your school considers it to be a benefit, an **Unlimited School License** will enable all school staff to use these programs (at school and at home; see more information attached).

Thanks!

© 2000-2015
All rights reserved
Original programs available at
www.fonts4teachers.com
info@downhillpublishing.com
(800)203 0612

Made in the USA
Columbia, SC
20 May 2022